HHH

Hetch Hetchy Haiku

By
Jennifer Fosgate

DANCING IMAGE STUDIO

Publisher:
CreateSpace Independent Publishing Platform
An Amazon company

Dedicated
to
John Muir

Crossing the divide
Stomach tight at sight I see
O'Shaughnessy

Melting stream of snow
Wapama falls to its death
From rock face above

The Harlequins bloom
Along the Hetch Hetchy trail
They see the sadness

My footsteps take me
Across concrete out of place
Sad Kolana weeps

Above sweet mist falls
Happy Tueeulala
Below submerged rock

First time I see it
Yosemite's drown valley
The ache is still there

Busy with people
Yosemite summer day
Hetch Hetchy so quiet

Under deep water
The Tuolumne still flows
Crying for the sun

How could this happen?
Granite valley water clear
The Hetch Hetchy lost

Yosemite's twin
This valley makes my heart sing
But a dam brings tears

Tuolumne's water
Dark over the drowned valley
Clear below the dam

The river laughing
Below O'Shaughnessy
Free at last to flow

The pens of Congress
Their ink is dark flood waters
Hetch Hetchy can't breathe

Our Yosemite
What if there was another?
Look under water

Wapama's waters
Wash me as I cross the bridge
They cleanse the sadness

Drive to Hetch Hetchy
A traffic jam will never be
This paradise lost

Let us right this wrong
See the river flowing free
Hetch Hetchy Valley

Tueeulala
The reservoir drinks your tears
Stop this sadness now

A postcard request
Kolana and Wapama?
There are none to buy

Great joy yet sorrow
This was Hetch Hetchy Valley
A damaged beauty

Lake you cannot swim
Valley floor you cannot walk
Hetch Hetchy problems

We the people stand
On a dam made of concrete
While Hetch Hetchy drowns

For additional information about Hetch Hetchy:

The website for Restore Hetch Hetchy contains history, photographs of the valley before being dammed, and restoration plans: hetchhetchy.org

Recommended reading:

"The Battle over Hetch Hetchy: America's most controversial dam and the birth of modern Environmentalism", by Robert W. Righter. Oxford University Press, c2005.

"Dam! Water, Power, Politics, and Preservation in Hetch Hetchy and Yosemite National Park", by John Warfield Simpson. Pantheon Books, c2005.

Hetch Hetchy Haiku is available at Amazon.com

www.ingramcontent.com/pod-product-compliance
Lightning Source LLC
Chambersburg PA
CBHW071257280526
45788CB00004B/1744